# Pollution

## Words by Herta S. Breiter
formerly Research Chemist
University of Illinois

RAINTREE
STECK-VAUGHN
LIBRARY
A Division of Steck-Vaughn Company

Cover Photo: Animals, Animals/Zig Leszcynski

Library of Congress Number: 87-23233

4  5  6  7  8  9   95  94  93  92  91

**Library of Congress Cataloging in Publication Data**

Breiter, Herta S.
  Pollution.

  Bibliography: p. 46
  Summary: Discusses various kinds of pollution,
their causes, and different ways to improve the
environment.
  1. Pollution—Environmental aspects—Juvenile
literature. [1. Pollution]  I. Title.
TD176.B73  1987        363.7′3        87-23233
ISBN 0-8172-3259-1 (lib. bdg.)
ISBN 0-8172-3284-2 (softcover)

# Pollution

sun

earth

All living things need the sun. They need light and heat from the sun. When the sun warms the soil, plants can grow in it. Animals need these plants for food. And people need plants in many ways. Nothing could live or grow without the sun.

Plants and animals that live in the sea also need the heat of the sun. The warm sea heats the air that is over it. The warm air brings water to the land as rain. The rain helps plants grow.

Only a thin layer of the earth is soil. Under the soil, the earth is mostly rock. Good soil and clean air are important to all living things.

The air, water, soil, and living things make up our environment.

Every day people are hurting the soil. Every day people are putting poisons into the air and water. We call this pollution. We must stop polluting our environment.

**glacier**

**plankton**      **fish**

All living things depend on one another. They are like links in a chain. If one link is killed, the others may die also.

In the Arctic near this glacier, tiny plants and animals called plankton live near the surface of the water. Fish eat the plankton. Seabirds come to eat the fish. If pollution kills the fish, these birds will starve.

sea gull

The seabirds nest on land. They leave droppings on the rocks. Mosses grow on the droppings. Later, other plants will grow on dead moss. Insects feed on the plants. Small animals feed on the insects. If the seabirds die, the other animals and plants will also die.

moss

fox

robin

badger

shrew

hedgehog

blackbird

hedge sparrows

Many kinds of animals, including insects, live near fields and in forests. The trees and bushes give them shelter. The insects feed on leaves, flowers, and seeds. Some birds and other animals eat the insects.

Sometimes farmers cut down trees and bushes. They do this to make room for crops. When they do this, they destroy the homes of these animals.

**Colorado beetles**

With no place to live, many of the wild plants and animals soon die. The farmer usually grows only one kind of plant in each field. So animals that feed on that kind of plant will have plenty of food. Such animals can destroy the crops. They are called pests. Many insects are pests.

Sometimes people do things that make the soil wash away. This is called erosion.

People cut down trees so grass would grow. Their animals pulled out all the plants. Soon all the plants were gone. There were no roots to hold down the soil. So the rain washed the soil away. Without soil, nothing much could grow.

There is a way to keep soil from washing away. Farmers can build terraces. The fields on them are small. They catch rain and hold it in the soil. So the soil does not wash away.

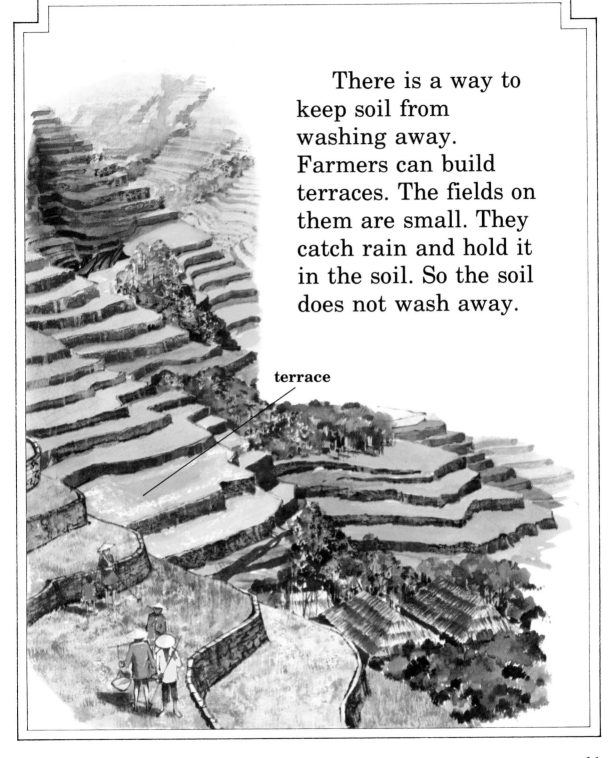

terrace

irrigation

spreading fertilizer

spraying pests

All over the world more people are being born every day. Farmers must find ways to grow food for all the people. Farmers can irrigate new land. They can add fertilizers to make plants grow better. They can spray their crops to kill pests. They can grow bigger kinds of crops.

barley

hawk

robin

caterpillar

spraying
caterpillars

Using sprays can cause pollution problems. Some sprays that farmers use to kill pests can harm useful animals. Small birds might eat pests that have been sprayed. The chemicals from the spray stay inside the body of the bird. A bird that eats such birds will also be poisoned by the spray. And its eggs will have thin shells that will break.

Air pollution is also a big problem. We often breathe dirty air. Some of the dirt comes from factories and houses that burn gas, coal, and oil. These fuels make smoke. They also can form a sulfur gas that can harm people and plants.

Many places have laws that keep people from making smoke. They must use fuels that don't make smoke. The factories must use filters to catch gases and dirt. But some gases still escape and pollute the air.

Cars pollute the air. The exhaust from cars can form smog. Smog is a mixture of smoke and fog. Smog can hurt people's eyes and lungs. Today all cars must have special devices that reduce the poisons that are in exhaust. But car pollution is still a problem because there are so many more new cars built each year.

Japan is trying to
control pollution. Its
scientists put caged rats
by the edge of busy
streets. If the rats die,
that means that the air
is very bad. It means
the air will hurt the
people. Some people
wear masks. Some
people get fresh air
from a special machine.

The smog and smoke from cars and factories are made up of gases and tiny bits of dirt.

Smog and smoke can spoil the paint on buildings.

Polluted air can poison the rain. The gases in the air form an acid in the rainwater. This acid can spoil stone and other building materials.

Polluted air can spoil farm crops. It can kill trees. If there is a lot of pollution in the air, less light and heat from the sun reaches the earth.

Cars are polluting the air of big cities.
So people must find other ways to move
about. Many big cities have subways.
Subway trains carry many people under the
streets. Buses run on the streets above. One
bus can carry as many people as fifty
cars can.

Some places won't let people bring their cars to the center of town. They must leave their cars at the edge of town in a parking lot. Buses bring them from the parking lot to the center of town. With no cars around, people can walk safely from place to place.

Noise is a kind of
pollution. Very loud
noise can make people
sick. Noise can hurt
your ears and spoil
your hearing.

Pollution hurts some people more than others. In some cities, there is not enough room for everybody. So some people live in slums. Slums are crowded, dirty places. Slums hurt the health of people who live there.

slums

Junk and garbage cause pollution. Things that people throw away are either junk or garbage. Some of these things rot.

Food will rot if thrown away. Things made of metal and paper also rot after a long time. But plastic and rubber never rot. They give off a poisonous gas when burned. So a big problem is finding a way to get rid of plastic and rubber junk.

Junk and garbage can be used to fill a pit. They are packed together and then covered with soil. But there are not enough pits for all the things people throw away.

People are now finding ways of treating old metals, glass, cloth, and paper so that they can be used again. This treatment is called recycling. Recycling helps to keep things from being used up too fast.

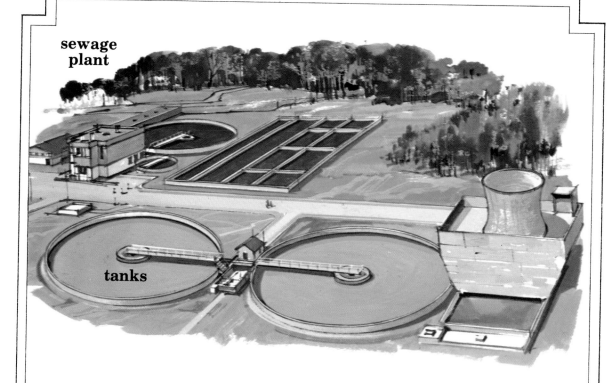

sewage plant

tanks

People send wastewater, or sewage, back to rivers and lakes. It is too dirty to go right to a river or lake. So it is changed at a sewage plant.

At the plant, the sewage goes through screens. The screens catch solid things. The rest of the sewage then flows into big tanks. The dirt drops to the bottom of the tanks. And the sun and air help kill the germs in the water at the top of the tank.

Many towns use water from this river. Wastewater is cleaned in sewage plants before it is dumped into the river. If wastewater is not cleaned, the river can become polluted with poisons and germs. The water finally flows into the ocean.

When warm water is put into rivers, it can cause thermal pollution. Thermal means hot. Hot water has less oxygen than colder water. Some fish cannot live in warmer water.

People are trying to save the
environment. They have set aside some
lands where only plants and animals can
live. No one is allowed to bother the
animals. No one is allowed to hurt the
plants. Here, living things enjoy their
natural home.

Some people have homes that depend only on nature. This is such a home. The people who live here collect rainwater for drinking and washing. Their sewage is collected in tanks. It is used later as fertilizer for plants. This sewage also gives off gas. The gas is used for cooking. This house gets heat from the sun. And the greenhouse gives the family food in winter.

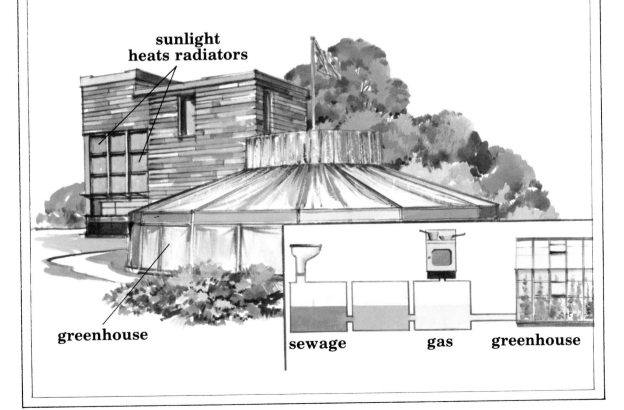

sunlight
heats radiators

greenhouse

sewage          gas          greenhouse

Plants and animals live in balance. This means they help each other. This picture shows how water plants and animals live together in balance. Each living thing gets all it needs from the environment.

snail

fish

The plants give food to the snails and fishes. They also put oxygen into the water. The animals must take in this oxygen to live. When they do this, they breathe out carbon dioxide gas. Plants then use this carbon dioxide to make food. This is how animals help plants.

minnow

The snails keep the aquarium clean. They help the balance by eating dead leaves and the droppings of fishes. An aquarium like this usually stays clean. But if the water becomes cloudy, it must be changed.

You can help your environment. You can start a compost heap to help your garden. A compost heap is a pile of food scraps, leaves, and anything else that will rot. You can also put weeds and grass clippings on the heap. Put water on the heap to help it rot. After a few weeks, spread the compost around your garden.

Some people help the environment by feeding birds. They put food on a bird table. They do this in cold weather. Birds have trouble finding food in winter.

If you feed birds, throw some food on the ground. Some birds like to feed on the ground. Watch how different birds eat.

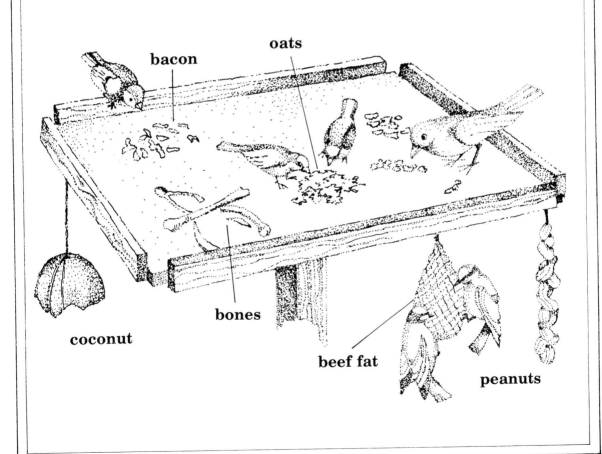

bacon

oats

coconut

bones

beef fat

peanuts

# The Metric System

In the United States, things are measured in inches, pounds, quarts, and so on. That system is called the American system. Most other countries of the world use centimeters, kilograms, and liters to measure those things. That system is called the metric system.

At one time the United States was going to change to the metric system. That is why you will see both systems of measurement in some books. For example, you might see a sentence like this: "That bicycle wheel is 27 inches (69 centimeters) across."

Most books you use will have only one system of measurement. You may want to change from one system to the other. The chart on the next page will help you.

All you have to do is multiply the unit of measurement in Column 1 by the number in Column 2. Your answer will be the unit in Column 3.

Suppose you want to change 15 centimeters to inches. First, find *centimeters* in Column 1. Next, multiply 15 times .4. The answer you get is 6. So, 15 centimeters equal 6 inches.

| Column 1 | Column 2 | Column 3 |
|:---:|:---:|:---:|
| THIS UNIT OF MEASUREMENT | TIMES THIS NUMBER | GIVES THIS UNIT OF MEASUREMENT |
| inches | 2.54 | centimeters |
| feet | 30. | centimeters |
| feet | .3 | meters |
| yards | .9 | meters |
| miles | 1.6 | kilometers |
| ounces | 28. | grams |
| pounds | .45 | kilograms |
| fluid ounces | .03 | liters |
| pints | .47 | liters |
| quarts | .95 | liters |
| gallons | 3.8 | liters |
| | | |
| centimeters | .4 | inches |
| meters | 1.1 | yards |
| kilometers | .6 | miles |
| grams | .035 | ounces |
| kilograms | 2.2 | pounds |
| liters | 33.8 | fluid ounces |
| liters | 2.1 | pints |
| liters | 1.06 | quarts |
| liters | .26 | gallons |

# Where to Read About Pollution

# Pronunciation Key

| | |
|---|---|
| a | a as in **cat**, **bad** |
| ā | a as in **able**, ai as in **train**, ay as in **play** |
| ä | a as in **father**, **car**, o as in **cot** |
| e | e as in **bend**, **yet** |
| ē | e as in **me**, ee as in **feel**, ea as in **beat**, ie as in **piece**, y as in **heavy** |
| i | i as in **in**, **pig**, e as in **pocket** |
| ī | i as in **ice**, **time**, ie as in **tie**, y as in **my** |
| o | o as in **top**, a as in **watch** |
| ō | o as in **old**, oa as in **goat**, ow as in **slow**, oe as in **toe** |
| ô | o as in **cloth**, au as in **caught**, aw as in **paw**, a as in **all** |
| oo | oo as in **good**, u as in **put** |
| o͞o | oo as in **tool**, ue as in **blue** |
| oi | oi as in **oil**, oy as in **toy** |
| ou | ou as in **out**, ow as in **plow** |
| u | u as in **up**, **gun**, o as in **other** |
| ur | ur as in **fur**, er as in **person**, ir as in **bird**, or as in **work** |
| yo͞o | u as in **use**, ew as in **few** |
| ə | a as in **again**, e as in **broken**, i as in **pencil**, o as in **attention**, u as in **surprise** |
| ch | ch as in **such** |
| ng | ng as in **sing** |
| sh | sh as in **shell**, **wish** |
| th | th as in **three**, **bath** |
| <u>th</u> | th as in **that**, **together** |

# GLOSSARY

These words are defined the way they are used in this book

**acid** (as′ id)  a chemical that has a sour taste

**aquarium** (ə kwer′ ē əm)  a glass container in which fish and other water animals can be kept

**Arctic** (ärk′ tik)  the area near the North Pole

**balance** (bal′ əns)  a way of living in which plants and animals help each other so that life is good for all

**bother** (bo<u>th</u>′ ər)  to annoy someone or something; to make nervous

**carbon dioxide** (kär′ bən  dī ok′ sīd)  a gas that comes from humans and animals when they breathe out; carbon dioxide is also given off when some things rot. Carbon dioxide goes into the air and is then taken in by plants and used as food.

**center** (sen′ tər) the middle of something

**chemical** (kem′ i kəl) a substance used in chemistry

**coal** (kōl) a hard, black fuel that is burned to give heat energy

**collect** (kə lekt′) to bring together in one place

**compost heap** (käm′ pōst hēp) a pile of rotted plants and other things, used as a fertilizer to make things grow better

**depend** (di pend′) to rely on; to trust in something

**destroy** (di stroi′) to ruin or kill something

**engine** (en′ jən) a machine that changes energy into force that can do work

**environment** (en vī′ rən mənt) all the conditions, or parts, of life that a person lives in, including air, water, soil, and all living things

**erosion** (i rō′ zhən) to wear away slowly

by the action of water or wind

**escape** (es kāp′) to get away from
   something or someplace

**factory** (fak′ tər ē) a building or group
   of buildings where things are made

**fertilizer** (furt′ əl ī′ zər) something
   that is put on soil so that plants will
   grow better

**filter** (fil′ tər) a device that lets water
   flow through but holds back solid things

**fuel** (fyo͞o′ əl) something that gives heat
   energy when it is burned

**garbage** (gär′ bij) waste; things that are
   not wanted

**gas** (gas) a fluid that is not a solid and
   not a liquid

**gasoline** (gas ə lēn′) a liquid fuel used
   in cars, trucks, and other things that
   have gasoline engines

**germ** (jurm) a small living thing that
   can be harmful to plants, animals,
   or humans

**glacier** (glā′ shər)  a large body of ice that moves slowly down a hill

**greenhouse** (grēn′ hous)  a building made mostly of glass where plants are grown

**insect** (in′ sekt)  a small bug that has three body parts and six legs

**irrigate** (ir′ ə gāt)  to bring water to a section of farmland

**junk** (jungk)  trash; garbage; something that is not wanted

**layer** (lā′ ər)  one thickness or fold of something that is lying over another

**lung** (lung)  the part of the body that makes humans and animals breathe

**machine** (mə shēn′)  a device that makes work easier

**mask** (mask)  things worn on the face to protect a person from bad air

**material** (mə tir′ ē əl)  the substance or mixture of things that something can be made of

**metal** (met′ əl)  a hard material that holds heat and carries electricity

**moss** (môs)  a plant that often grows like a blanket on something

**natural** (nach′ ə rəl)  a place or way of living that is what a person or animal is used to. Living free is natural to animals; living in a zoo is not natural to animals.

**nature** (nā′ chər)  the whole world; an animal's or human's natural place

**oil** (oil)  a liquid fuel that is burned for its heat energy

**oxygen** (ok′ sə jən)  one of the gases in the air. All plants and animals must have oxygen to live.

**pest** (pest)  something that annoys or bothers

**pit** (pit)  a hole in the ground

**plankton** (plangk′ tən)  groups of tiny plants and animals that float on water and are food for fish

**plastic** (plas′ tik)  a material made by humans and used in objects such as bags, pens, electric plugs, and many other things

**poison** (poiz′ ən)  something that harms or kills a living thing

**pollution** (pə lo͞o′ shən)  things that make the environment unclean

**problem** (prob′ ləm)  something that is puzzling; a mystery

**recycle** (rē sī′ kəl)  to use something again; for example, old tin cans can be treated and used over again as new cans

**screen** (skrēn)  a device that is used as a filter to stop solid things from passing through

**seabird** (sē′ burd)  a bird that lives near a sea or ocean

**sewage** (so͞o′ ij)  waste that is carried away by sewers

**slum** (slum)  an area in a city or town that often has too many people, bad housing, and poor conditions

**smog** (smog)  a mixture of smoke and fog

**snail** (snāl)  a small, slow-moving animal that has a hard shell

**soil** (soil)  the top layer of earth

**special** (spesh' əl)  something that is not common; unusual

**spoil** (spoil)  to ruin; to damage

**spray** (sprā)  a jet of tiny, flying drops of water or other liquid

**subway** (sub' wā)  an underground tunnel in which a train that carries people runs

**sulfur** (sul' fər)  a chemical that gives off harmful gases when it is burned

**terrace** (ter' is)  a flat area of land that has a steep drop, usually to another flat area of land. Terraces help prevent erosion.

**traffic** (traf' ik)  the movement of cars, trucks, and other vehicles

**treat** (trēt)  to do something to a thing in order to change that thing

**waste** (wāst)  something that is thrown away; something that cannot be used

# Bibliography

Gutnick, Martin J. *Ecology*. New York: Franklin Watts, 1984.

Hammer, Trudy J. *Water Resources*. New York: Franklin Watts, 1985.

Lampton, Christopher. *Planet Earth*. New York: Franklin Watts, 1982.

Milne, Lorus J. *The Mystery of the Bog Forest*. New York: Dodd, Mead & Co., 1984.

Oda, Hidetomo. *Insects in the Pond*. Milwaukee: Raintree Publishers, 1986.

Stone, Lynn M. *Marshes and Wetlands*. Chicago: Childrens Press, 1983.

Swanson, Glen. *Oil and Water*. Englewood Cliffs, New Jersey: Prentice-Hall, 1981.